D0786576

Bel the Weather Girl

RAINDROPS ON A ROLLER COASTER

HAIL

BELINDA JENSEN
illustrated by Renée Kurilla
series consultant: Lisa Bullard

Ⓜ Millbrook Press/Minneapolis

To all of the curious, earnest, sincere seven year olds in Salt Lake City and Minnesota who welcomed me into their classrooms with my slide projector for over twenty years to talk weather. "Joe the Hailstone" was the story that blossomed into this whole project. —B.J.

For my good friend Hannah, whose admirable enthusiasm for science is a lot like Bel's —R.K.

Millbrook Press
A division of Lerner Publishing Group, Inc.
241 First Avenue North
Minneapolis, MN 55401 USA

For reading levels and more information, look up this title at www.lernerbooks.com.

Polka dot background: © Wiktoria Pawlak/Shutterstock.com.

Main body text set in ChurchwardSamoa Regular 15/18.
Typeface provided by Chank.

Library of Congress Cataloging-in-Publication Data

Jensen, Belinda, author.
    Raindrops on a Roller Coaster: Hail / by Belinda Jensen ; Renée Kurilla, illustrator.
        pages cm — (Bel the Weather Girl)
    Includes bibliographical references and index.
    Summary: Bel and her cousin, Dylan, explore hail, learning about when and how hail forms.
    Audience: 005-007.
    Audience: K to Grade 3.
    ISBN 978-1-4677-7958-6 (lb : alk. paper) — ISBN 978-1-4677-9747-4 (pb : alk. paper) —
ISBN 978-1-4677-9748-1 (eb pdf)
    1. Hail—Juvenile literature. I. Kurilla, Renée, illustrator. II. Title.
QC929.H15.J465 2015
551.57'87—dc23   2015015838

Manufactured in the United States of America
1 - CG - 12/31/15

TABLE OF CONTENTS

Chapter One
Summer Storm

Bel felt a drop on her cheek. She glanced up. Dark clouds blocked the sun. Lightning zigzagged in the distance. Bel wasn't afraid. But she knew she'd be safer in the house.

Tall, heavy clouds, called cumulonimbus, become thunderstorms. These clouds are filled with rain. It makes them a dark color.

"Looks like a storm is coming," she said to her cousin Dylan. "We'd better head inside." Dylan ran for the door with Bel's dog, Stormy. Bel followed.

BOOM!

Thunder rumbled. Rain pattered against the windows. Bel looked for Dylan and Stormy. Then she spotted Stormy's tail.

WEATHER ALERT!

A meteorologist studies and predicts the weather.

6

Bel ducked down next to Dylan. "I know you're afraid of storms," she said. "But remember, Mom's a meteorologist. She knows what to do to stay safe, even if we aren't under the table!"

Chapter Two

Ice Fall!

Something began banging on the roof. "Uh-oh! Stormy and I think we should stay under here," said Dylan. "At least until the house stops falling down."

"Dylan, look, you don't want to miss this!" Bel pointed outside. Small ice balls bounced onto the yard. They pinged off the swing set. "The house isn't falling. Hail is!"

Hail sounds loud and scary, but hail-related injuries are not common. People are usually safe inside a building.

"Ice in the middle of summer?" asked Dylan.

Hailstorms happen during warmer months, not during the winter.

"They're called hailstones," said Bel. "Hail sometimes falls during thunderstorms. I'll tell you all about it. Weather isn't so scary once you understand it!"

COLD

WARM

Chapter Three
Swirling Raindrops

"Storm clouds are full of rain and wind." Bel zoomed her arms up. "Sometimes the wind carries raindrops to the tops of the clouds."

"It's cold up there," Bel added. "So the raindrops get an icy jacket. They turn into tiny balls of ice. Then they start to swirl around in the wind."

brrr!

The tops of tall storm clouds are usually made of ice. When the storm winds are strong, they carry raindrops up to this icy layer. Water freezes at around 32°F (0°C).

Bel continued. "The balls of ice keep swirling around inside the cloud. They get another icy jacket each time the wind makes them fly up again. Sometimes the ice balls stick together. They make bigger, lumpier balls."

"So how do they end up down here?" asked Dylan.

Bel looked around. A bag of frozen peas sat on the counter. Bel grabbed some peas. She circled them through the air. Then she dropped them to the floor.

PLUNK!

"The ice balls get too heavy for the wind to keep them up. Then they fall to the ground. That's hail. Most hailstones are small, like these peas. But in storms with tons of wind, the hail swirls in the cloud a long time. Then you can get hail almost as big as this soccer ball!"

A record-breaking hailstone fell in South Dakota in 2010. It was 8 inches (20 cm) across and more than 18 inches (46 cm) around. But huge hail is very rare.

Bel's mom smiled at Dylan. "The good news is hailstorms last just a few minutes." She pointed outside. "See, the storm has been done for a while. Let's go out and take a closer look at some hailstones."

Mom cut the biggest hailstone in half. It had rings inside like the rings in a tree trunk. "Each ring is another jacket of ice," said Mom.

Safety tips: Make sure a storm has completely passed before going on a hailstone hunt. Only adults should cut open hailstones. They will need a sharp knife.

Chapter Four

Raindrops on a Ride

Dylan kicked the soccer ball. "That's why I call you Bel the Weather Girl. You know all about the weather! So hail is just raindrops on an icy roller coaster? I guess I didn't have to take cover under the table. Of course, that was all Stormy's idea!"

Wheeee!

Bel grinned. "You're right about hail, but stay tuned for tomorrow.
Because every day is another weather day!"

Try It: Measuring Melt

Hailstones fall during warm weather, so it doesn't take long for them to disappear. But just how fast do they melt?

You won't often get the chance to test a real hailstone. So for this activity, you'll use an ice cube instead!

What you will need:

Paper

Pencil

Any thermometer that can determine the temperature of the room

Cloth tape measure

Ice cube (leave it in a freezer until you are ready to use it)

Paper towel

Timer

What to do:

1. Use your paper and pencil to make a table that looks like this:

Time	Room temperature	Ice cube size

2. Write down the time and the room temperature in the correct spaces on the top line of your table.

3. Wrap the measuring tape around the ice cube. Write down the ice cube size in the correct space on the top line of your table.

4. Leave the ice cube sitting on the paper towel.

5. You are going to measure your ice cube again every few minutes to see how much it has melted. If you started with a large ice cube, measure it every 15 minutes. If it is a small ice cube, measure it every 5 minutes. Set your timer for the correct amount of time.

6. Measure your ice cube again when the timer goes off. Make sure to wrap the measuring tape around the ice cube the same direction you did the first time. Fill out another line of your table.

7. Set the timer again for the next measurement. If you started with 5 minutes but there was very little change in the ice cube, increase the amount of time.

8. Continue to fill out your table until your ice cube is gone. How long did it take to melt?

Glossary

cumulonimbus: a high-towering cloud that often produces rain and storms

hailstones: balls of ice that form in clouds during warm-weather storms

hailstorms: storms during which hail falls

meteorologist: a person who is trained to study and predict the weather

Further Reading

Books

Higgins, Nadia. *It's Hailing!* Edina, MN: Abdo, 2010.
This title will teach you more about hail.

Mezzanotte, Jim. *Hailstorms.* Pleasantville, NY: Gareth Stevens, 2010.
This book gives you a chance to see photos of hailstones while learning more about these storms.

Websites

Exploring Earth

http://www.classzone.com/books/earth_science/terc/content/visualizations/es1805/es1805page01.cfm?chapter_no=visualization
You can watch an animation of hail forming at this website.

Tree House Weather Kids: Hail

http://urbanext.illinois.edu/treehouse/clouds.cfm?Slide=10
This website includes an audio clip to help you learn more about hailstorms.

Weather Report for Kids

http://kidsweatherreport.com/
Enter your zip code and see weather forecasts in your area for today and tomorrow.

Index